Dear Mary Ann

Titles in this series:

Dear Mary Ann

Carol Christian

MACMILLAN
PUBLISHERS

Introduction

Do you read magazines? Teenage magazines? There are usually lots of different things to read: stories, pop music, fashion, sports, letters etc. Many people like to read the problem page in a magazine – to read about other people's problems, and to read the answers the magazine gives.

'Dear Mary Ann' is the name of the problem page in a teenage magazine called *Teen Scene*, and in this story we meet some of the boys and girls who read the magazine, and who write to 'Mary Ann' about their problems.

Dear Mary Ann

Carol Christian

MACMILLAN
PUBLISHERS

First published 1991
Reprinted 1994

Published by
MACMILLAN PUBLISHERS LIMITED
London and Basingstoke

Illustrated by Pat Nessling

Cover design and illustration by Indent, Reading

Typeset by Macmillan Production Limited

Printed in Malaysia

A CIP catalogue record for this book is available from
the British Library.

ISBN 0-333-51256 1

Contents

Introduction

Do you read magazines? Teenage magazines? There are usually lots of different things to read: stories, pop music, fashion, sports, letters etc. Many people like to read the problem page in a magazine – to read about other people's problems, and to read the answers the magazine gives.

'Dear Mary Ann' is the name of the problem page in a teenage magazine called *Teen Scene*, and in this story we meet some of the boys and girls who read the magazine, and who write to 'Mary Ann' about their problems.

1 Dear Mary Ann

There's a new paper on the news stands. Everyone at our school reads it. It's called *Teen Scene* and it's for teenagers. That's people from thirteen to eighteen years old.

Teen Scene has a lot of stories and pictures. It has news and puzzles and jokes. There's a sports page and a music page, and a page for people who collect things. There's a page about television and films. There's something for everyone.

I like the letters page. Half of the page is called *Dear Mary Ann*. There's a photo of Mary Ann at the top. She looks friendly and nice. People write letters to Mary Ann and tell her their problems. Do you have any problems? Mary Ann gives good advice.

Sometimes the letters are funny, but sometimes they are really sad. Most of my friends don't read them. That's what they say, anyway. I know it's not the truth. They just read them when no one is looking.

My friend Adam buys *Teen Scene* every week. It comes out on Tuesday and he buys it from a shop after school. He gives it to me on Wednesday or Thursday. Everyone else reads it before me, but I don't care.

Belinda, the girl next door, gets her *Teen Scene* at home. The paper boy brings it to the house every Tuesday morning. I know, because I see him. He puts it in the letter box. Belinda's lucky. My father won't order it for me. My father is my problem!

Adam lives in our street, too, at number fifty-four. He's sixteen and he's on the football team. My brother's on the team, too. He and Adam are the same age. Adam plays

football with my brother and me after school, in the big field behind our house. I'm thirteen and my name is Pete. Belinda is fifteen. She and Adam are not friends, but Belinda sees Adam at school. All the girls watch Adam at football games. He moves fast! When he gets the ball, the girls all stand up and shout, 'Come on, Adam! Come on!' Our school did well at football last year. Adam scored most of the goals.

Teen Scene is a very good paper. There is a story with pictures on the front page. It's a comic strip, but *Teen Scene* isn't just a comic. The stories are really good. Can you believe it? My father reads them when no one is looking. Then he says, 'Teenage comics are a waste of time'.

The back page is full of games and puzzles. There are word puzzles, picture puzzles, and number puzzles. I like the number puzzles best.

I'm going to be a reporter some day and write stories for the newspapers and television. I don't talk much but I listen a lot. I keep my eyes and ears open. I'm writing some stories now. Do you want to read them? The stories are true.

2 Belinda and Tracy

It all started on a Tuesday, about a month ago. Belinda walked to school with her friend Tracy, as usual. On Tuesdays they don't talk very much. Belinda reads her copy of *Teen Scene* and shows it to Tracy.

'Can I read it after school?' Tracy asked.

'No, you can't,' Belinda told her. 'I'm sorry.'

'Why not?' asked Tracy.

'I'm going to do the puzzles after school. Why don't you buy a copy, Tracy? It's very cheap. It's only forty-five pence.'

'I haven't got forty-five pence,' answered Tracy, 'but Mother gives me pocket money on Saturday. I can buy it next Tuesday.'

Belinda turned a page of the paper. 'Okay,' she said. 'You can read it tomorrow, after I finish it. *Dear Mary Ann* looks interesting. There's a letter from a girl called Julia. She wants to be a pop star.'

'I want to be a pop star, too . . . with green hair and gold eyelashes and a silver dress,' said Tracy. Tracy always talks like that. 'What does Mary Ann's letter say?'

'I don't know yet.' Belinda laughed and turned another page of *Teen Scene*. 'She probably asks "Can you sing, Julia?" You can't sing a note, Tracy! But do you want a silver dress? On page five it shows you how to make one.'

'I'm going to make a skirt,' said Tracy. 'I want a new skirt for the school party.'

Belinda said, 'Here you are! There's something about food on page five, too. You can read it tomorrow. Then you can make some food *and* a skirt for the party.'

Tracy took the copy of Teen Scene from Belinda. She looked quickly at page five. '*Party food: make it in a minute!*' she read.

Then she giggled. 'I can't make food in a minute. I can't make food in an hour. I can't cook. My mother cooks the meals in our house.'

Belinda said, 'I cook the dinner sometimes but I can't sew. I can't make a skirt. My mother is always sewing. She makes my skirts and dresses.'

Tracy giggled again. She giggles a lot. 'I've got an idea,' she said. 'Why don't we write a letter to Mary Ann, Belinda? We can say this:

Dear Mary Ann
    We are two schoolgirls. We read *Teen Scene* every week. But one of us can't cook and the other one can't sew. We have no boy friends. What shall we do?
    Love,
        Belinda and Tracy

Belinda laughed. 'Don't write the letter. I can tell you the answer. I read *Dear Mary Ann* every week. She always says the same kind of things.'

'Tell me, then. What's she going to say? What's the answer to our problem?' asked Tracy.

Belinda thought for a moment. Then she said:

Dear Belinda and Tracy
    Thank you for your letter. Don't worry. I can't cook either, but I have a boy friend. He likes to cook and he is always hungry. He's a good cook. Sometimes he cooks the dinner.
    Some boys like to sew, too. Do the things you like to do. Boys usually do that.
        Best wishes from your friend,
        Mary Ann

3   Adam and his friends

Adam and his friends, Ben and Simon, went into town after school. Adam bought *Teen Scene* at the newsagents and showed it to his friends.

'Why do you spend your money on that paper every week?' Ben asked. He took the silver paper off a bar of chocolate and began to eat it. 'I never read newspapers. We read lots of books at school. Do you want some chocolate, either of you?'

'No, thanks. I want to keep fit for the next game. A lot of chocolate isn't good for you,' replied Adam.

'Thanks. I'd like some,' said Simon. He held out his hand.

'I buy *Teen Scene* because there are so many good things in it,' said Adam. 'I always read the sports page. Look here, on page six. One of the big football clubs has a player who is only seventeen. I'd like to play football for a club like Arsenal.'

'Show me,' said Ben. Adam showed him page six and waited. Ben looked at it. Then he turned to the back page.

'I want to look at the answers to the crossword puzzle,' he said. 'I can usually solve it but last week I couldn't get the answer to 9 Down. I thought it was *letter*, but it's *better*.'

Simon looked over Adam's shoulder. 'I like the music page. You can read all about the new releases. There are pictures of pop stars. I'm going to write and ask for that photo of Madonna. Did you see the charts this week, Ben?'

'No,' said Ben.

Simon looked at Ben. Then he took the paper from

Dear Mary Ann

Adam and turned it to page four. 'Maybe you'd like the *Do It Yourself* page,' he told Ben. 'You can learn how to make things. You don't need to read. Just follow the pictures.'

'That's a nice little table,' added Adam. 'You can make it in a day.'

'Not me!' said Ben.

'It's not expensive, either. You can buy the wood for five pounds.'

'I haven't got five pounds,' said Ben.

Simon said, 'You're not much fun, Ben. Don't you like to make things? I do. I'm going to make that table. After that, I'm going to make a frame for the picture of Madonna.'

Adam grinned at Ben. 'You don't like to read and you don't like music and you don't like to make things. What do you like?'

'He likes girls,' said Simon.

'Girls? What are they?' Adam laughed and patted Ben's shoulder. 'How's your love life, then?' he asked.

Ben looked unhappy. 'Bad,' he said. 'I like girls but they don't like me. That beautiful girl in our French class never even looks at me. I'd like to pull her hair sometimes, I get so angry.'

'That's too bad,' said Adam. 'Why don't you write a letter to Mary Ann? Maybe she can help. Look. There's a letter right here from a boy called Michael.' He read the letter to his two friends.

Dear Mary Ann

I like girls but they never notice me. What can I do? I'm sixteen years old and I'm six feet tall. I have dark hair and dark eyes and I don't wear glasses. My face isn't bad. I've got good teeth and I clean them every day. My face and hands are usually clean. My shoes are not very dirty.

My clothes are nothing to write home about but they're okay. Everybody wears jeans at our school. I'm quiet but I'm friendly.

Dear Mary Ann

I am sending you my picture. Is anything wrong with me? I worry about it.

Yours sincerely,

Michael

'Poor Michael!' said Ben. 'What does Mary Ann say? Is there an answer to his letter?'

'Yes. Read it. She always gives good advice,' said Adam. Ben read the letter to his friends.

Dear Michael

Thank you for your letter and the photo of yourself. Don't worry. Nothing is wrong with you. You look fine.

A lot of boys worry about girls, so you are not the only one. Most boys want to have a girl friend. Everyone wants love.

Perhaps the girls are not interested in you at the moment. Sometimes, at your age, girls feel more comfortable with other girls. They are not very sure of themselves yet. Cheer up. Smile at the world. Things are going to change. I know it. You're going to get a big surprise.

Best wishes from your friend

Mary Ann

Ben gave the paper back to Adam. 'Well! What help is that? Michael wants a girl friend. How can he get one? That's what he wants to know. Does the letter tell him? No, it doesn't.'

'Mary Ann tells him to cheer up and grow up,' said Simon. 'That sounds like good advice to me. It might help you, Ben. You look like a dog without a bone.'

Ben still looked unhappy. 'Well, I don't believe everything I read in the newspapers. I'm not crazy like you two. Who on earth is this Mary Ann?' he asked. 'Who is Michael?'

'They aren't friends of ours,' said Simon. 'We can't tell you. We don't know.'

Dear Mary Ann

'I do,' said Ben. 'Teenagers don't write these letters. Someone in the office at *Teen Scene* writes them. A fat old man with dark glasses and hot hands. He sits down every morning and pretends he is a teenager. He dreams up a few problems and writes the letters. He signs them with different names — Michael, Sarah, Alice, Jack . . . Then he writes the replies.'

'No, he doesn't', said Adam. His voice sounded angry. 'Mary Ann is a girl. She's quite young. That's her picture at the top of the page. Look.' He showed Ben the photo. Then he folded the paper and put it in his pocket. 'That's Mary Ann.'

Ben just laughed.

That night Adam wrote a letter to Mary Ann.

Dear Mary Ann

I read *Teen Scene* every week and I usually read *Dear Mary Ann*. You understand teenagers and give them very good advice.

I feel sorry for the letter-writers because they are unhappy, but I don't understand them. They are young and they live in a good country. They go to good schools. Why can't they stand on their own two feet?

Don't they have mothers and fathers? Don't they have teachers? Don't they have friends? Why do they write to you and ask so many silly questions?

Yes, I know. I'm asking silly questions too. What I really want to know is this. Do young people write those letters or do you write them? My friend says, 'There is no Mary Ann. A fat old man with dark glasses writes the letters. He writes the replies too.'

Please tell me, is that true? Who are you, Mary Ann?

Yours sincerely,
Adam

4 Adam and Belinda

One Tuesday afternoon, Adam went into the town by himself. He bought his paper and then he went and stood at the bus stop. He was tired after a football match against another school.

Belinda was at the bus stop, too. She had her guitar with her. She has guitar lessons on Tuesdays. Belinda looked really nice in a new red dress. Adam noticed her for the first time. She hid behind her copy of *Teen Scene*.

Adam hid behind his paper for a few minutes, too. Then he said, 'Hello, Belinda.'

Belinda looked up from the paper and smiled. He knew her name. That was a surprise.

'Hello,' she replied. 'You're Adam, the football player. I watched the match this afternoon. You did well. Do you read *Teen Scene* every week?'

'Yes, I do,' said Adam. 'I like the sports page.'

'I like *Dear Mary Ann*,' said Belinda. 'There's a letter today from a boy called Adam.'

'Yes, I know,' said Adam. 'That's me. I wrote it.'

'Did you? Is that letter from you? Honestly? I don't believe it. It's such a funny letter.' Belinda started to laugh. Then she saw his face. He looked hurt and unhappy. 'Oh, I'm sorry!' she said. She turned away and picked up her guitar.

The bus came at last and Belinda got on. She looked back at Adam. When she saw his face, she started to laugh again. She couldn't stop.

Adam didn't get on the bus. He stood for a moment. Then he started to walk home. He felt angry. What was so

funny about his letter to Mary Ann? Why did Belinda laugh at it?

He stopped walking and read the letter again. Then he read the reply from Mary Ann.

> Dear Adam
>
> Most teenagers are unhappy sometimes. They fall in love. They don't tell anyone, because they don't want people to laugh at them.
>
> They tell me about it, instead. Sometimes I can help. Is everything okay in your life, Adam? If it is, that's fine. You don't need my advice, but some people do.
>
> I promise you, I'm not a fat old man with dark glasses. I'm a young woman. That's my picture in the paper. I certainly don't write the letters. I just read them and write the answers.
>
> Best wishes from your friend,
> Mary Ann

Belinda saw Tracy on the bus and sat down beside her. 'Hi!' she said. She began to laugh again.

'Hello, Belinda,' said Tracy. 'What are you laughing at? Tell me the joke.'

Belinda replied, 'Oh, Tracy! I'm laughing because I'm happy. I'm happy because I'm in love. I'm in love with Adam, the football player. Did you see him at the bus stop? Isn't he wonderful? He called me by my name.'

'You look pretty today,' said Tracy. 'I like your red dress. Boys like red, too. Is Adam in love with you and your red dress?'

'I don't know,' said Belinda. 'He probably doesn't even like me. He didn't get on the bus. He's angry because I laughed at him. I laughed because he wrote this funny letter to Mary Ann, in *Teen Scene*. Look, Tracy. Here it is. Isn't it funny?'

Belinda showed Tracy the letter. They laughed and giggled all the way home.

Adam was tired and angry and he had a long walk home.

On the way he met Ben and the beautiful girl from his French class. Her name is Helen. Ben looked cheerful. He grinned at Adam and said, in a friendly way, 'Hello. How's everything?'

Adam was really unhappy. He nodded but he couldn't speak. He walked past Ben and Helen and didn't say a word.

Adam went straight to his room when he got home. He got out his pen and wrote a letter.

> Dear Mary Ann
> Now I understand what you mean. I'm unhappy too, because I'm in love for the first time. I can't tell my friends, so I'm telling you. The girl is fifteen and her name is Belinda. She reads *Teen Scene*. Today she looked lovely in a beautiful red dress. She comes to all our football games, but she thinks I'm a joke. She laughs at me.
> What can I do?
> Yours sincerely,
> Adam

The next Tuesday, Adam played in a football match against another school. Belinda and Tracy watched the game from the sidelines. Everyone from our school was there. I sat next to the girls. Adam looked up when the team came onto the field. He saw us there.

'What are you smiling about now?' Tracy asked Belinda.

Belinda opened her copy of *Teen Scene*. 'Look at this, Tracy. There's a letter to *Dear Mary Ann* from Adam. Can you believe it? And Mary Ann's reply is very good. She knows exactly what happened. She understands why I laughed at Adam.'

The letter said:

> Dear Adam
> It hurts when people laugh at you, but remember this. Sometimes girls laugh at boys because they like

them. Some people just laugh when they are in love. Why is Belinda laughing at you? Do you know? Did you ask her? Be brave. Don't run away. Her answer isn't going to ruin your life.
      Your friend,
      Mary Ann

Adam scored two goals in the first half of the game. Everyone cheered. Tracy and Belinda stood up and chanted, over and over. 'Who scored the goal? Adam! Adam! Who's our hero? Adam! Adam!'

We got worried in the second half when the other school scored twice. Tracy shut her eyes. 'I can't watch,' she said. 'I'm going to *die* if our team doesn't win!'

'Me, too,' agreed Belinda. Then my brother kicked the ball in for our third goal. The whole crowd cheered like mad.

Our school won the game by three goals to two. Belinda looked very happy. 'I'm not laughing at Adam. I'm just laughing,' she told Tracy. 'I'm really proud of him.'

As Adam came off the field, he looked towards us. Belinda waved her *Teen Scene* in the air and laughed.

Adam walked away with the rest of the team. He didn't laugh. He just put his hand on my brother's shoulder and smiled.

5   Martin and Lucy

Adam and Belinda are great friends now. They go every-where together. At first, people teased them a lot. Everybody knew about the letters to Mary Ann, and people made jokes. Now nobody thinks about it any more.

I like reading letters from my friends in *Teen Scene*. But most of the letters to Mary Ann come from people I don't know. Sometimes they write lovely letters and I feel I'd like to know them. A lot of them have big problems that really hurt. The problems we have look small beside theirs.

There was one from a girl called Lucy . . .

Dear Mary Ann

Four years ago a black family moved into the house next to ours. They're really nice and the children are the same age as my brother and me. Their grand-mother and grandfather live with them.

The grandfather and grandmother came to England from Trinidad, but the rest of the family were born in England. They're good neighbours and they're British like us, except they're black.

Serena and I are in the same class at school. We do our homework together, and we go to a dancing class on Saturdays. Her brother Martin and my brother were in the same class, too, but they are both working now.

Martin passed his driving test when he was seven-teen. Then, on his eighteenth birthday, his grand-father gave him an old banger. Last week, he invited me to a party.

I said, 'I'd love to go,' but my mother says 'No.' She won't say why. 'I am not a baby,' I said. 'After all, I am sixteen.'

Of course, I know why she doesn't want me to go. It's because he's black. She likes Martin, so she won't say so. I am so angry! How can I tell him? What shall I do?

> Best wishes,
> Lucy

Mary Ann replied:

Dear Lucy

Thank you for your letter. I read it several times and I thought about it a lot. It's an old story and a sad one. Juliet's family and Romeo's tried to keep them apart.

I can't solve your problem, but you can. Think hard about it. Talk to your mother and Martin. You don't want to hurt either of them, so it's not easy. But you must talk together.

Be honest. Tell them how you feel. Don't tell lies. Talk bravely and honestly and tell the truth. Help them to speak the truth, too.

I can't think of any other answer.

> Your friend,
> Mary Ann

The day those letters appeared in *Teen Scene*, everyone at school talked about them. People had very different opinions.

Some people said Lucy was a fool. 'Aren't there enough white boys around?' they asked. 'Why does she want to go out with a black one?'

Other people thought Lucy was sixteen years old, and she could decide for herself. 'Why doesn't she just go to the party?' they asked. 'How can her mother stop her?'

Adam and Belinda nearly had a fight over it. Belinda

said, 'When you like people, it doesn't matter what colour they are. Lucy's right and her mother's wrong.'

Adam said, 'How do you know? Martin isn't at school now. He has grown-up friends. Maybe Martin and his friends do things Lucy's mother doesn't like. Maybe they drink a lot or take drugs. Maybe he's a bad driver. Maybe the car's not safe. Lucy should obey her mother.'

Ben heard him. 'It's easy to say that, Adam. You're not Martin. Belinda's mother lets her go out with you. Would she if you were black?'

'Martin's not poor, is he?' said Tracy. 'He's got a car and everything. Maybe he belongs to some funny religion.' She giggled. 'My father can't stand people with funny religions.'

Belinda's face was pink. 'I don't care what colour people are. I don't care what their religion is. I don't care what clothes they wear. If I love them, I love them!' she declared. She was almost in tears.

'Take it easy!' said Adam. 'Don't get hot and bothered. You're right, of course. I want to choose my friends, too. I don't want my parents to choose them. But life isn't that simple, Belinda.' He put his arms around her.

Simon was there, too. He took a deep breath and looked very serious. 'Does Lucy's brother take Serena to parties?' he asked. 'If not, why not?'

We all laughed, then. We didn't know Lucy or her neighbours but we had strong feelings about them. Until Simon spoke, we felt quite angry.

I can't tell you the end of this story, because I don't know it. Lucy didn't write to Mary Ann again. I hope she's happy. I hope she and Martin are still friends.

I have three pen friends. One is in Asia, one is in Africa, and one is in America. They write interesting letters. I have photos of them. They're all different colours and they have different religions. My father doesn't mind. Of course, it's not the same as Martin and Lucy. My friends live thousands of miles away.

6 The girl in the French class

One day, Ben said to Adam, 'Did you really write to Mary Ann? Everyone says so.'

Adam smiled. 'Don't believe everything people say,' he replied.

'And Belinda saw the letter and now she's your girl friend,' said Ben.

'That's right. It happened because we both read *Teen Scene*. But it can't happen to you because there isn't any girl called Mary Ann. You said so. A fat old man with hot hands writes the letters.'

Adam grinned. Then he saw Ben's face. Ben looked ill. His face was almost green.

'What's the matter, Ben? Did I say the wrong thing?' he asked.

'No, but I need Mary Ann's advice. I still think it's a silly idea, but I need help. I have a problem and I must tell someone. I can't do my school work. I can't sleep at night.'

'That's bad,' said Adam. 'Tell me, if you want to. I can keep my mouth shut. Did you fight with Helen? Doesn't she love you any more?'

Ben shook his head. 'Oh, no. That's not the problem. She loves me very much — and *that* is the problem. I can't get away from her. She never leaves me alone. I don't see my friends. I can't work on my stamp collection.' He shook his head again. 'I don't want to talk about it.'

'Well, write to Mary Ann, then. That's why she's there,' Adam told him. 'That's how she earns her money. Send her a letter.'

Ben made a sad face. 'Maybe I will. Simon said the same

thing. It sounds crazy to me, but maybe I will.'

Every week, Adam looked for Ben's letter. He never found it. Then one Tuesday there was a strange letter to Mary Ann. Adam showed it to Belinda. 'What do you think of this?' he asked her.

> Dear Mary Ann
> There's an awful boy in our school. His name is Ben and he thinks he is God's gift to the girls. He often looks unhappy, like a dog without a bone, and the girls feel sorry for him. One girl likes him a lot and follows him around. She is in our French class.
> He liked her at first, but now he's bored. He can't get away from her. She wants to be with him every minute of the day.
> Isn't he awful? He likes girls until they fall in love with him. Then he doesn't like them any more. Tell your readers to be careful of boys like that. Boys like that can break their hearts.
> Yours sincerely,
> Caroline

'I don't know any girl called Caroline,' said Belinda. 'It can't be anyone at our school.'

'Does any girl follow Ben around, so that he can never get away from her?' Adam asked.

'The one in our French class does, but her name's Helen.'

They thought for a moment. Then Belinda's eyes opened wide. Adam nodded his head. 'Caroline's not the real name of the girl who wrote the letter,' they said, both at once.

They looked at Mary Ann's reply.

> Dear Caroline
> You are right. Some people chase girls for fun. They don't really love them. Ben is just playing a game, like a cat with a mouse. Show this letter to the girl in your French class. Ben is afraid to tell her the truth.

It's a waste of time to follow boys like Ben around.
Choose some other boy and make eyes at him! And
cheer up. There are plenty of boys.
        Best wishes from your friend,
        Mary Ann

Belinda looked wise. 'Mary Ann knows,' she said. 'The
girl in the French class wrote the letter. Look at the last
three lines. Mary Ann speaks straight to her.'

When Ben met them after school, he looked quite cheerful. Adam asked, 'Did you write to Mary Ann?'

'Why do you ask?' said Ben.

'We are wondering,' said Adam. 'There's a strange
letter in *Teen Scene* today.'

'Did Helen write it?' asked Belinda. 'It's from a girl
called Caroline, but it sounds like Helen. We just won-
dered.'

Ben read the letter. He thought hard for a moment.
Then he shook his head. 'I wonder, too,' he said. 'Does it
really sound like Helen? Does Helen say things like that
about me? They're not very nice.'

'She's not following you around today,' said Adam. 'I
don't see her. Do you?'

'Well, you know what girls are like,' said Ben, with a
grin. 'One moment they love you madly. The next moment
they don't love you at all.'

Adam looked closely at his friend. 'Be honest, Ben. Did
you write to Mary Ann?' he said again.

Ben laughed. 'Call me Caroline,' he said. He winked at
Belinda. 'She knows how awful boys are.'

~ ∎ ~

Helen dropped Ben like a hot brick. She has another boy
friend now. Ben still likes the girls, but he doesn't have a
special girl friend. He gets *Teen Scene* and reads the Stamp
Collectors page. The funny thing is, the girls still like Ben!
I don't understand it. Do you?

Dear Mary Ann

I'm Pete, your story-teller. Remember? I'm not going to write to Mary Ann about anything. I'm happy the way I am. I watch my friends and listen to them, then I write stories about them.

Exercises

Dear Mary Ann

1 Who is Mary Ann?

2 Who is telling the story?

Belinda and Tracy

3 Why does Tracy want to read Belinda's magazine?

4 What problems do the two girls have?

Adam and his friends

5 Does Ben like to read newspapers? Why/why not?

6 What is Ben's problem?

7 What does Ben think of Mary Ann?

Adam and Belinda

8 Why is Adam angry?

9 Why does Belinda smile the next time she reads *Teen Scene*?

Martin and Lucy

10 What is Lucy's problem?

11 What does Mary Ann say about Lucy's problem?

The girl in the French class

12 What is Ben's problem now?

13 What does he do?

Glossary

7   *releases* (n):   new records
     'You can read about the new releases . . . on the
     music page.'

20   ***Romeo and Juliet***:   two young lovers in a play by
     William Shakespeare, whose families would not allow
     them to marry
     'Juliet's family and Romeo's tried to keep them
     apart.'

Language Grading in the Macmillan Bookshelf Series

This reader has been written using a loosely controlled range of language structures. There is no tight control of vocabulary as it is based on the authors' experience of the kind of vocabulary range expected at each particular language level. The authors have also taken care to contextualise any unfamiliar words, which are further explained in the glossary. We hope you will try to deduce meaning from the context, and will use a dictionary where necessary to expand your lexical knowledge.

The language items listed here show those most commonly used at each level in the **Bookshelf** series:

Level One (elementary)
Mainly simple and compound sentences, beginning to use more complex sentences but with limited use of sub clauses

Present Simple	Positive and negative statements
Present Continuous	Interrogative
(present and future reference)	Imperative
Past Continuous	And, or, but, so, because, before, after
'Going to' future	Some/any (-thing)
Past Simple	Basic adjectives
(regular and a few common irregular)	Some common adverbs
Can (ability)	'Simple' comparatives, superlatives
Would like (offer, request)	Gerunds/infinitives, common verbs

Level Two (lower intermediate)
Simple and compound sentences, limited use of complex sentences

Present Perfect	Conditional, can, could (possibility)
Will/won't future	When/while
Present/Past Simple Passive	Question tags, reflexives
Have to, must, should, could	Comparatives, superlatives
Can/may (requests/permission)	(common adjectives/adverbs)
Infinitives (like, want, try, etc.)	Reported speech (present/past)
Gerunds (start, finish, after, like, etc.)	

Level Three (intermediate)
More complex sentences, including embedded clauses

Present Perfect Continuous	Conditionals 1 and 2
Past Perfect	Although, to/in order to, since
Present/Past Continuous Passives	(reason)
Perfect Passives	So/neither
Ought to	Reported statements, requests, etc.
May/might (possibility)	

Level Four (upper intermediate)
At this stage there is minimal control, although authors generally avoid unnecessary complexity

Future Continuous	More complex passives
Past Perfect Continuous	Conditionals 3